Haunt

Mark Granier

salmonpoetry

Published in 2015 by
Salmon Poetry
Cliffs of Moher, County Clare, Ireland
Website: www.salmonpoetry.com
Email: info@salmonpoetry.com

Copyright © Mark Granier, 2015

ISBN 978-1-910669-01-3

All rights reserved. No part of this publication may be reproduced or transmitted in any form or by any means, electronic or mechanical, including photography, recording, or any information storage or retrieval system, without permission in writing from the publisher. The book is sold subject to the condition that it shall not, by way of trade or otherwise, be lent, resold or otherwise circulated without the publisher's prior consent in any form of binding or cover other than that in which it is published and without a similar condition, including this condition, being imposed on the subsequent purchaser.

COVER PHOTOGRAPH: *Mark Granier*
COVER DESIGN & TYPESETTING: *Siobhán Hutson*
Printed in Ireland by Sprint Print

*Salmon Poetry gratefully acknowledges the support of
The Arts Council / An Chomhairle Ealaoín*

in memory of my mother, Sheila Granier, 1918-2012

Acknowledgments

Acknowledgements are due to the following print and online publications where some of these poems, or versions of them, first appeared: *B O D Y*, *The Irish Times*, *The New Statesman*, *The Yellow Nib*, *Poetry Ireland Review* 100, *The Moth*, *Burning Bush 2*, *Magma*, *The Workshop*, *The London Column*, *Ink, Sweat & Tears*, *Kritya Poetry Festival Anthology*, '*And Other Poems*', *The Horizon Review*, *The Stony Thursday Book*, *The Morning Star* and *Poetry Review*.

Some of these poems also appeared in the following anthologies: *In Their Own Words: Contemporary Poets On Their Poetry* (Salt, 2012), *The Robin Hood Book: 131 Poets In Support of the Robin Hood Tax* (Comparison, 2012), *In Memoriam: Poems Of Bereavement* (Candlestick Press, 2012) and *If Ever You Go: A Map Of Dublin In Poetry And Song* (Dedalus, 2013).

My special thanks to Séan Lysaght, Liam Ó Muirthile, George Szirtes, Peter Sirr and Chris Stevens for their encouragement, valuable close readings and suggestions.

I am very grateful to the Trustees of the estate of Katherine Kavanagh for awarding me a Patrick and Katherine Kavanagh Fellowship in 2011, to Culture Ireland for a Travel Bursary in 2013 and to An Chomhairle Ealaíon/The Arts Council for a Literature Bursary in 2013.

Contents

Grip Stick	11
Bullseye	12
'How Far Is Outer Space?'	13
Academic	14
The Catch	20
A Fire Balloon For Luke	22
Haunt	24
Planet Y	25
Of A Man, Falling	26
Snow Set	27
Two Questions	28
Five Lizards	30
Bamboo	32
Ringsend	33
Travellers On Pigeon House Road	35
The Ballast Office	36
Open	38
Two Readings	39
Sips	40
Keys	41
Father's Day	42
Oscar's Grave	44
Late Addition To The Lament	45
Forever And Ever	46
Rockville	47
Sped	54
Funny Peculiar	55
Lillian's Dream	57
Neary's	58

Nope, I Haven't Yet Figured Out What Beauty Is For	59
Unanswers	60
Stopping For The Twelve Apostles	62
High Rise Squat, 1989	64
The Tents	65
Stolpersteine	66
The Rice Lady	67
New York Stopover	68
The Crawling Hand	69
Time Piece	70
Present Continuous	71
Primaries	72
The Reverse	75
Tweet	76
Paintings In A Room	77
For Goya's Dog	78
Lost Lens	79
Evening Sun, Bullock Harbour	80
Tat	81
Some Like It	82
Thigh Gap	83
Holdall	84
Navels	85
Vulture Bone Flute	87
Hairpin	88
Cochlear Implant	89
Boy On A Trampoline	90
Notes	92

Grip Stick

The man emptying bins on the prom might be my age,
though healthier looking, tanned, bare-armed
in a hi-vis jacket and black ski-cap.
He plucks at stray bits of litter with that familiar
metal rod with its Dalek pincer — the same

as the one I bought for my mother in Fannin's
some years before she died — a gadget
so starkly ingenious surely it's a branch
of a family tree of similar inventions, of Bakelite,
whalebone, leather, wood… going back, back

to that afternoon in her nursing home
a year and a half ago, when I hold her hand
and feel it loosen then go slack, and call
the nurse, who says quietly 'yes, she's going…'
and I look out the window

to see the usual glorious rubbish, clouds
not stopping their tumble over Killiney Hill's
huddle of slates and satellite dishes, while I am
abruptly in a different country — the vast
landscape of her open palm —

tiny in the grip of what gave way.

Bullseye

Spiddal at dusk, in the rear-view a grainy swirl
over the rooftops — starlings? — that murmuration
I'd hoped to witness. Swerving, pulling in
under the copse near the church, I saw

what it was: rooks, their cries
sharp as springs bursting from the sky's mattress —
a murderous parliament swelling, shrinking, circling
the tattered wind of itself, black

as the trees taking them back,
coming in low so my upturned face felt
the fury, and a single hard tap
on my shoulder could only be

that species of luck, accuracy.

'How Far Is Outer Space?'

If you take a car and aim it
straight up you can arrive in under an hour
without breaking the national speed limit.

But first, you will need to find the right
car, my broken-in, grey-blue 323
with the James Bond pop-up headlights.

Comfortable as a pair of old trousers, those trips
when I pulled hedged-in nightscapes
around me, up to my hips.

No CD or airbag, though you can allow
your airbag mind to inflate, fill every crevice
from the foot-well to the rear window.

Gun the angle, push the stick all the way
into vertical, flick on the high beams
and you're away, a bulging roar

of dust in gravity's layby.

Academic

> *School's out for summer*
> *School's out forever*
> *School's been blown to pieces*
> —Alice Cooper

Kindergarten

A grey house lost in a big field
is 'the German school'. Herr Schmidt's eye-patch is real.
Herr Müller does not smile.

During break I learn how to slot together two dry
stalks of horse chestnut leaves — the bones
of an airplane. When I try

the new noise on my tongue, it gets stuck
in my teeth, though I can count from null
to elf, and bid Guten morgen, Gute nacht —

Merit Cards

Stiff, with rounded edges, like invitation cards,
there are three kinds, three colours.

The best, to say you are doing good work or great,
is pink as a strawberry milkshake.

My later ones, anaemic blue, carry 'Remarks'
such as my mother's 'I'd like to see higher marks.'

The rarest, iodine yellow, you can almost smell:
mitching? stealing? — one stop from being expelled.

Headmaster

There is his specially made
leather 'biffer' — hand-sewn for the trade?
He calls it Lizzy, and there is a Big Lizzy too.

He has his eye on me, on you,
'gurriers' in our army coats of 'bull's wool'.
When he warns 'There'll be wigs on the green'

my blankness flickers, screens
some antique scuffle: a lawn, powdered rugs
flying from what must be our own heads

done up as Ladies, M'Luds.

Chemistry

The lovely wrongness of mercury.
I ask Paddy where we can get some, so

he asks the Japanese boy, Sato,
who escorts us into the empty lab

as if he owns it. We tip
a whole Aspirin bottle's worth out of a tube

and before we can wonder
what to do with it, Paddy — in secret communion

with some inner double-dare — rolls
one of those molten heavyweight pearls

off his palm onto his tongue.

Confirmation

How difficult can it be?
Transubstantiation? The Trinity?'

But when the soft face under the tall hat mouths
'Who made the world?' it wafer-melts

into its echo: the one test
you could not fail to pass, or digest.

Latin

Mr Banks' drone could not be drier
as he conjugates: amo, amas, amat…
till a terrible drought rolls in along the Tiber,
the flagons empty, love itself gone flat.

English

'I wandered lonely…' as Gardner (Weedy)
passing our window — in his hands
a book held open like a breviary.

Poetry, since now and then he'll chance
on a nugget and halt to tilt his face
at the sun: a practiced smile, *radiance*.

French

Mr Feutren (Fruity) isn't from France
but Brittany. Important. Make no mistake.
Something — anger? passion? — has shorn his face
to a bald, beak-nosed, hunched-electric presence.

Yes, he fought with the SS during the war.
A Breton nationalist, why should he hide
what he believes? What he did was justified
(though I'm not sure who these justifications are for).

The Irish, so *stupide*! Hard to believe
how little we know, and how can we make a start
when, in restaurants, we ignore the hearts
of artichokes, to nibble at the leaves.

Now he has lost patience and swoops to wrench
some slowcoach from his desk. I am in his sights
and will be next. Because of (or despite)
whatever he fled, he teaches excellent French.

BIOLOGY

On a wall in the jacks: I am 13 and I love gees —
'The penis is then placed in the vagina…' —

breaking the seal, entering the soft-lit harem
in a smuggled *Penthouse* (all those misted women) —

but when a 5th year boy unfolds a page of these
close-ups — cunts in lurid mugshots — we've skipped

to a field manual, a dressing of wounds, ripped.

RUGGER

A door swings open or shut
for good, when in the midst of it
I discover I've laced my new, unbroken boots
to the wrong feet.

Coláiste Na Rinne: An Interrogation

— Ar dhúirt tú rud mar gheall ar shite?
— Ní dhúirt mé.
— Dhúirt tú.
— Ní dhúirt mé.
— Dhúirt tú.
— Ní dhúirt mé.

— Dúirt!

[…]

— Scríobh!

Break

— da-Ding, da-Ding, da-Ding
                              the hand-held bell
swarms us onto the concrete, voices up
and over the high stone wall —

Get up the yard! I'll swop you…   Whew, just saved!
What's white and moves quickly across the floor?
What's the definition of agony?
Show us your steely! I've heard that before.
Quickly, which would you rather be
nearly-drowned-or-nearly-saved

— da-Ding, da-Ding, da-Ding

A Reading

No matter if you're a dosser or a swot,
when asked to read a poem aloud the protocol
is to sound like a bored robot —

then Kinsella's Garden on the Point
where 'the speckled bean breaks open' and 'the snail
winces and waits', and the brunt

of some odd imperative pushes me ahead
of myself, to brace my elbows, cover my ears
and read it, for once, the way it should be read.

The Catch

Not a team player, even in a team of one,
I could rarely conscript myself
to that sweeping aside, great clear-felling of woes,

though I admired the way the oval ball
got reborn, wobbling out
from a thicket of muddy legs,

or how soccer's untouchable orb — shrunk to a bright
dot on the duplicate screens —
touched like a bolt, brought the lounge to its feet,

and sometimes, channel-surfing,
I fell in with Wimbledon's sharp little grunts and thwacks
that made of the air something

furiously lashed and strung, harp of lines
firm enough to climb
to a kind of music: swing, kick, dance

out of civilised skin, into
instinct and brilliance — worn green oblongs shot through
with jazzy, doodling grace notes, raptures

of disappointment, even their own
concise stretches of boredom boggy and grey
as infinity — yet the lovely

footloose physics of it all
somehow seemed less riveting
than table soccer or slot-machines in Pierre's Pool Hall.

Something in me backed off
from gladiatorial ecstasies, or preferred them
filtered by distance: my high-ceilinged,

mouldy bedsit on Mountjoy suddenly aired
by one of those windy roars — a ball missed
or saved in nearby Croker —

to which I raise a toast: Here's
to the maker of whatever happened or didn't, the catch
in drifts of silence, cheers.

A Fire Balloon For Luke
— on his non-confirmation day

They open it — tall husk
of a paper lampshade —
in the midst of the garden's
midsummer dusk

where it's buffeted
by unseasonable wind
while we shield and feed it
a procession of snuffed

candles, lighters, till yes!
waxed cross-wires at the base
catch and breathe
yellowness

we take great care
to release, as if part of us
were learning to walk
tipsily on air:

eye-level, then aloof
skimming the bone-dry
bushes, Scots pines,
a neighbour's roof:

fluttery heart,
secular flourish
with a numinous flavour,
a life we can chart

holds us as it sways, shrinks
and dawdles over
the indigo hill
where it winks

to a black flake
of particulate
matter: a micro-
ache.

Haunt

Grandfather, you were the man of the house,
the one who slacked the fire and rose at dawn
to poke it into life, a waking pulse.

You hated night-lights burning, would come down
in your stockinged feet, to flick the Bakelite switch:
our whispers in solid dark, abruptly drowned.

So I find myself, back in the old-fashioned kitchen
of the place you bought (and we sold) — a fitting home,
though I was far too absent to know it then.

Sheets on the indoor washing line. I part them
to see the door already swinging open,
the moment closing in, trailing its hem.

Is a ghost any less a ghost if it's a dream?
You're tired, slightly stooped in your wine-red jumper,
grey sides of your bald head slick with Brylcreem.

Our eyes don't meet. I know why we are here:
for you to begin again, retell each story
and me to finally listen, and remember.

I rifle the nearest dresser drawer (the one
with rubber gloves, corks, scissors, snarls of twine...)
for a pencil stub and anything to write on.

You sigh, ask for 'a cup of tea', and I take
those words down as the dream-silt stirs and dims
and muddles me awake.

Planet Y

At five he tells us 'you can choose when you die,
you go to the Dying Spot and jump in.'

Later, going to bed, he has questions
our careful answers cannot begin to satisfy.

So he tells us what he hopes for, a planet where
we wake after we die: its laws

that nobody dies and there is no school 'because
everyone knows everything.'

Some nights, you can almost bring it in focus,
a furiously coloured-in dot

that might be a dead pixel, a flaw in the glass
or might not.

Of A Man, Falling

At-ease-looking, almost poised —
though his soiled shirt

has come untucked — he might
be attempting to pass

the one-leg-stand test
or lounging, between drinks,

at a party, his back
braced by a wall, if

the world had not turned
him upside down

into the plummet
of streetwindowsky,

the brain in its cockpit — flight
the flight of his thought

a ten second freight —
for all we know

a counterweight.

Snow Set

Caked shoes
                croaking the new-laid road,
I like to look up and into it
                        above iglooed cars, lobed
branches and wires
                feel it curious
on ear, eyelash — try to
                separate the dots, see through
the thicker cloud-crumbs:
                air filming itself
tinier and tinier,
                negatives of the night sky
ashily sliding, restlessness
                    fused with silence
putting things calmly,
                calmly awry.

Two Questions

How Does The Water Bear

fare
where there is neither air
nor water

unless astute

nature
made for
a creature far
less than a drop of water

a space suit
?

What?

Nothing, nada,
down the plughole with Dada,

entropy
finally getting stroppy,

The Great Duckegg, cosmic shrug
pulling the rug

on which old Schrodinger's cat
shat,

not even a screed,
scatter of stars, birdseed,

sprinklings of nowt
but a pocket turned inside out,

squat,
not a jot,

dot
   dot
      dot

Five Lizards

1. BENIDORM 1966

It could let go its tail if caught.

Fat siesta sun full
on my back, I kept still, held
myself invisible, in love
with its dry archaeological scuttle

quicker than thought.

2. SILVES 2001

Those two, geckos with the magic toes —
guardians of our rented house
in Portugal. While we watched

the terrible loops of data on CNN —
the towers turned
into blooming smoky candles again and again —

they returned each night and set
under the porch light
short delicate shadows.

3. MALAGA 2004

When you threw another log on the fire
something half-fell, half-

scrambled, smoking on the hearth.
Must have been asleep in the woodpile. For

a handful of heartbeats it froze
as if considering — flagstones, open door

to the Andalusian stars —
before skittering back to its bolt-hole, the core

raftered with blue-orange flame —
safe as ashes, as clay,

already part of the same
sky we'd be vapouring into the following day.

4. Inis Mór 2005

Saw a sand lizard's face poke
out of a slice

of blackness in a gryke
and was vouchsafed

something of the island's discrete
micro-climates — time zones

seeded between the old
carboniferous floors

shifting their scales —
elaborate flying buttress

of bramble and tiny, rare
nova-flowers that burn

in there with feathery tails
of maidenhair fern.

Bamboo

They've planted a low-maintenance Mohawk wall
along the drive to his school.
In blustery November, ashen stalks
click their fingers and walk
the wind through its steps — feathery plumes
shiver and flounce with each shock

that ripples into waves — fields of industrial crops:
breadbaskets, whole continents
where the dance is unconstrained
as a tribe of unbroken horses tossing their manes:
borderless movements that will lift
and set a person's gaze winging, adrift.

Ringsend

The Gaelic language was prohibited along with Gaelic dress —
saffron-dyed clothing, moustaches, long hair and forelocks.
    JOHN O'BEIRNE RANELAGH, *A Short History of Ireland*

Point of the tide, spit of land, An Rinn
where you spoke the tongue, rode bareback, lay
low, outside the city walls; The Green
Patch where The Dodder and The Liffey

bled into the sea's industry — air
briny and clean off the wrinkled sand or it swings
from the lower circles, sulphur —
end of the moorings, iron rings

threaded with ropes, the crew ashore
drinking at the sign of The Good Woman,
a fanlight intact or gone in above the hall door,
rum, cotton, coffee, tobacco, resin…

the city dump smoothing its dunes
shaken by raucous gulls to a snow-globe
where hand-to-mouth, ragged platoons
stumble, stoop, probe

for anything, a gleam like a ring in barmbrack,
the recycled riddle
crunching a razor-shell — container ships, stacks
of bibles and ironsides, landfill-

name that reclaims itself, sings, begets
lorries, caravans, tidal traffic —
from The Salmon Pool to the light on Poolbeg — nets
and net curtains, shipshape village of red brick,

Quality Row, Whiskey Row, drone
of dirt bikes revving near the Waste Water Treatment Plant
buffered by the bird sanctuary's green zone —
a Brent Goose, a wing-stretching cormorant —

ebbing bay-wide emptiness, the bare scroll
cloud-lit, in a steady state
of arrival, where a solitary soul
with bucket and spade, digging for bait,

pauses, as a Sealink ferry slides out
past the Pigeon House, landmark
chimneys ringed red & white,
steamboat funnels, making of the land an ark

with washing strung on a high-
security fence (her blouse the forbidden saffron):
what a grey or blue or green or brown eye,
departing, will look back on.

Travellers On Pigeon House Road

Some years now, since they were moved on
by a long acre of boulders set down
magisterially as glacial erratics.

Driving the bay side, where drifts of sand
lap the road like a desiccated sea,
I used call on Arthur and Margaret

who would make me at home, serve tea
while their two youngest girls on the beach played house
with an old carpet, a battered suite of furniture.

Near the scrap metal dock, Billy's and Mary's
was like a miniature garden centre: wicker chairs,
a ceramic Laurel & Hardy, potted plants.

I never got round to calling on the others, near
the lorry-thundering roundabout, their curtains
flickering blue: a TV's phantom hearth.

Ranged behind them: a ditch, a barbed-wire fence,
security cameras, enormous silent cranes
and neat aisles of well-travelled steel boxes

bigger than caravans, containing next
to anything (furniture, foodstuff, TVs
bound for homes or business parks), oblongs

of what we'll soon have in common: securely sealed
absences of light numbered in rows
lived-with and familiar as a neighbour's field.

The Ballast Office

i.m. John Pidgeon

Plash of oars — where are we going
with this? John and his son Ned are rowing

their customers through an eighteenth century
sea mist shifting slightly

off the sloblands between Ringsend
and where we can set foot on dryish land:

stone blocks being laid
for The Great South Wall. Lemonade

ale and good food ahoy — a wooden shape
unmoving, not a ship

but the Blockhouse,
Pidgeon's place, where we'll dock.

*

Family scattered, the name
holds on for hotel, barracks, power station,

lengthens for Pigeon House Road — parallel
with the East Link Toll —

over miles of what was marshland before the Liffey
narrowed for Rogerson's Quay,

for The Ulysses, The Swift, top-heavy
cruise and container ships, clanking Ro-Ro ferries,

bulk cargo unloading on the north docks
where the nightwatch fox

sinks its paws in the maize, leaves a blurred loop
of tracks on the shifting slope.

*

Ballast, the Office of things holding their own —
the lighthouse, the traffic cone,

the sooty redbricked shell
of a factory whose post-industrial

shadows are cooped in the rafters:
his name spelt in heralding wing-beats, feathers

and beyond it the fogged, wobbly, piercing blip
of a light-ship

that rose, steadied to a squat lighthouse, red
as the light it blinks: starboard

for outgoing vessels or anyone taking a stroll
to the end of The South Bull.

Open

said the handmade sign
(underscored by a red arrow)
inside a doorway one step
from a Soho street. We stopped
just a tick, then longer, as if
we had some business here

other than letting our eyes
travel the strip-lit grey
narrowing walls, torn lino,
lines draining like a sink
to a high arch, behind which
steel-edged stairs further the lesson

in perspectives: the whoosh of
compressed centuries, a lost
hunting cry, razzmatazz, brass
rubbings of jazz, appetite's
arrows, taxies and here's
one now —

Two Readings

No one has read my palm.
I won't let them.

Not that I believe those lines
more meaningful than canals
on Mars, but to display
the soft pink valleys, how they
might read to a strange-eyed stranger —

'The life-line's fractured
and there seems to be…' 'What?' 'No, nothing.'

And how long's a *frayed* piece of string?

*

Now, examining them closely

under the reading lamp,
I tilt them this way and that,
as if the official stamp

of age — overscored lines
crosshatching into a fine
scrollwork of loosening nets —

might be a forgery.

Sips

My mother needs to drink three jugfuls of water
which is just as difficult as it ought to be
when your 93-year-old bones are spiteful
with osteoarthritis. 'Just keep taking small sips'
I say, though I know well

that in this desert water is far from ambrosial.
If I lifted the sky, blew off the sand like dust,
I'd uncover her stooped over a stream — water
dark as the unruly hair falling in her eyes,
while she cups handfuls

deliciously cold after the climb above some hazy
post-war city (Munich, Belfast, Rome…)
whose busy streets have no room, no corner
for a 54-year-old son who keeps telling her
to take small sips.

Keys

At 18, I wore a bunch of them — pendants
on a leather thong. I wanted secrets

to keep, the jingle, the little teeth
turning the pins, old

tangible symbols. As if I might learn to belong
by playing at being warder

to a makeshift life: the front door
to my first home, Rockville (the only one

with an actual name); the flat
with a fire escape that stopped short

of tousled, fogbound gardens, a neighbour
calling her cat in 1974;

the padlock that released, from Stephen's Green,
one buckled bicycle wheel;

the cardboard and leather suitcase I inherited
from grandfather, who'd kept it

under his bed, perhaps so he could sleep
on old letters, tinted postcards,

a big brass paddle and key
to a hotel room high in The Windy City.

Father's Day

It seems, now, I will never find
your shoes, father, let alone fit in them,
though I still hope to follow the cold trail
of adventure in your smile, your spark
that landed me here, where
even though I am a father in my turn,
my footing is far from certain.

Rumours rustle in the visible
branches of my family tree. An uncle
traced you, found a married man. But no
he did not (or maybe it slipped his mind).
His daughter thought he once mentioned Medicine Hat —
Medicine Hat! Such a marvellous name
I tried it on for size, for a while.

A French Canadian soldier, my mother said,
neglecting to mention which war
claimed you, so I grew up thinking
World War Two, realising eventually
it ended a decade too early.
Tentative questions raised that flicker of pain,
slaps from a self-interrogation.

Have I other half-brothers? Sisters?
How many of your whip-tailed seeds made it home?
I suppose you're gone now, burned
or buried, dog-tagged in stone,
but until I can mark, encircle
that appearing-vanishing point, you'll remain
enchanted, undead, prone, your face

furiously shifting and running, fast-
forwarding weather, the everyday
sky convoys, sea's military colours,
crowd-faces in the street, on TV, armies
of old men — all and none
remind me of you. My known
unknown, how have you shrunk, grown?

Oscar's Grave

*It is touching that they remember him with such affection.
But on the other hand it is really tiresome*
— MERLIN HOLLAND

Scrub off those lipstick kisses
pressed on the pale stone
and they'll return, shades
of pink, terracotta, snail grey.

Would he have blanched, haunted
by atrocious wallpaper?
Or seen the outline, an illustration
for some story he might —

if he could gather his thought:
a prince whose elegant name
deserted him, having stolen
the life he might have lived

and the death also, eyelids
breathed on, kissed closed.

A Late Addition To The Lament

He has drappit the mirk-daurk craig
on hummle, muckle Norman MacCaig:
his one-fag, two-fag, at lang-an-last three: —
Timor Mortis conturbat me.

For Ever And Ever
and for Simon and Nuala

He wanted to be piggybacked, a couple of hundred yards.
'Wait till we're nearer home.' 'But it's so far!'

So I asked if he remembered his grandmother's sister
who died last year. 'Nuala. Yes, I loved her.'

And did he know, every day, in her eighties, she'd walk
down to the café? 'On her own?' 'Of course.'

'And now', he said, 'she has gone away forever…'
'That's right.' But he hadn't finished: '…and ever and ever…'

And so on, all the way home, not at all sadly,
as if by chanting, hitting the same key,

he could turn something, or roll into place some stone
I might want to roll aside and carry him home.

Rockville

White and blue, simple lines —
the house where I was raised

aged like anyone, grew
a beard of Virginia creeper
whose feelers felt between frames.

Here is a place we might have kept
instead of being haunted by,
that is holding, to this day,

keystones — the air in those rooms.

*

In the top drawer, so different from
the soft, neatly folded clothes: her necklaces —
pearls and beads, the pink coral

trickle and click through my fingers — feel
the precise weight of the tangle
of memory and dream.

*

Cloakroom under the stairs

cools its heels. A waft
from its curtained alcove: old boots,
turps, Brasso, shoe polish,

blue and red lino, a narrow aisle
padded on one side
with the family's gallery of cloaks:

my mother's orange sheepskin
(from *One Million Years B.C.*),

grandfather's weathered mac
and trilby, the cocky, offwhite
golfer's cap (disapproved of),

grandmother's Persian lamb,
her mink stole's tiny paws
and hard-nosed, rodent faces

slow my travelling hand.

*

Above mum's bed, in an alcove, three plywood shelves
sag a little, like hammocks, under the weight
of Linda Goodman's *Sun Signs*, Belloc, Betjeman,
*A Child's Garden of Verses, Winnie The Pooh,
The Larousse Encyclopaedia of Greek Mythology,*
a Dream Dictionary (that warns against dreams
about weddings: funerals in disguise), James's Michener's
Iberia (grown-up, black and white photographs
of hot dust, sharp shadows, blood, sweat, age).
What else? *The Wind In The Willows, Leaves of Grass.*

*

The heavy-headed roses have grown
dishevelled, swaying above her

as she stoops with secateurs
among upright, woody stems, extravagant thorns,

burying, I once pompously wrote,
'her regret' (At what? Not having lived

a more ordered or wildly-lived life? Not being sure
of herself or what she should do?).

More likely just pleasuring, becoming lost in
velvety pinks, creams, carmines

curling like old photographs
tattered and edged here and there

with tea-brown stains.

*

Grandfather whacks at the hedge with a golf club:
at something inside: the cornered rat's
bloodied squeal, locked wheels,
metal biting on metal.

*

Grandmother half-folds her *Evening Press* and points
at something in Dubliner's Diary, The Gay Sweatshop:
'Mark, who are all these "gay" men? Why
are they so happy?'

*

The green ribbed trunk belonging to my uncles
lives on the landing, part of the house's time

machinery, heady aroma of old books, brass
and leather: a holster, a bullet casing, a tome

on forensic medicine (good for a dose of horror),
an agonised Christ's head carved from Plasticine,

a microscope, a stained-glass smear of blood,
a paperback of Sartre's *Intimacy*...

*

It isn't music moves me

to a Sellotaping frenzy,
smothering my wallpaper's

faded flowers with rock bands,
from *Sounds* and *Melody Maker*,
whose sounds I have yet to hear.

I like their serious eyes
and seriously long hair;
most of all, the names:
King Crimson, Black Sabbath, Curved Air…

On a different note, *Hannie Caulder*
in a cowboy hat and poncho
(airing her hip's bare curve)

is a bass chord, clearly heard.

*

Behind the drawing room,
the dimmer, colder dining room
looks north. Lunch on the table,
palms are steepled: 'Bless us
our Lord for these thy gifts…

Amen.' Not much else
is said, unless grandfather
drop-clatters his knife and fork
to storm through the French windows
with his old war cry: 'Get out of it!' —

flapping a great white serviette
at the barely disturbed birds
in the topmost branches, dining
on our apples and pears.

*

In his eighties, his poker-faced, dry-as-ash
response to 'How are you keeping, Mr MacAllister?'
is either 'I've got youth on my side' or
'Ach, one more clean shirt.'

*

Later the wasp sting, the stroke,
the photo no one took
in which he stands, at a loss on the back lawn:
'These are the dog days.'

Later still, in the kitchen,
alone with my cousin, he says:
'There is a ghost standing beside me.
I don't like him. Tell him to go away.'

*

I am summoned again, handed
the oil-dark scissors to clip
from behind his purple ears, the silvery eaves.

And again: bright summer evenings,
he sits hunched in the bath while I sponge
his bony, freckled shoulders.

Distances, hard words, words
that should have passed between us
here in the wash of light

through clouded glass, the comforting
faintly sour smell of the facecloth,
each echoey drop

of water on water — skin.

*

Removal: a grey day
buries itself briskly. In the coffin:

creased and set, the wax-&-iodine
kernel of his face.   Outside, afterwards,
an elderly nun is shaking everyone's hand:
'He was a warrior, he was a warrior…'

*

What changes (apart from something in the house
closing its artery)? Grandmother's quietness and privacy
and her wistful smile still plays

to my old elsewhereness. A new bedroom is made
of the downstairs 'study'. Hers becomes the spare
nobody sleeps in: cool, net-curtained light,
flowered curtains, a trace of face powder and lilac.

Surfacing from the first bout of pneumonia,
all she'll say is: 'It's a long story.'

*

Unable to sleep, I get up to open the window,
stop, take a step back. Directly below,

a streetlit silhouette (a man's) is standing still
as topiary, at the edge of the lawn. Unreal.

I wake my mother, to witness, verify:
'Probably some drunk spending a penny.'

When we peep again he's gone, leaving behind him
the *Now You See Me* cast from a dream or film.

Trespasser, drunk, thief with second thoughts
(or ghost of my half-named father, on and off),

I have your negative, sharp, perfectly framed,
where strange looks into strange.

*

Such sleepwalking, it seems hard to believe.

For instance, how is it neither of us notice
till late afternoon, grandfather's grandfather clock

has gone? How do we miss
the space at the bottom of the stairs
where (hollow, not even the ghost of a tock),
its tarnished brass face had outstared
itself in the black-framed mirror?

Slyly, early, before the household woke,
intruders had eased the front door,
not quite closing it on their departure —
but what quietly broke
our reverie, finally, was what they left
unroofed on the floor, a nested, neat

little square of dry leaves.

*

I sometimes open Google Earth, to plunge
through the exploded city into the green
of our old tree-bordered road, to hang

above the newer, expanded, sky-lit roof,
the front lawn long paved over, the roses gone
with the rockery, what was left of the wood-framed swing.

Closer, and it mosaics into pixels, tiles
implacable as the roof's blank pyramid
under which I've slithered to raid

this ramshackle orchard.

*

Here is the first foot
I have set at my grandparents' (now
also my mother's) grave
in Deansgrange, here the first flower
I lay on the stone: grandfather's
execration (somewhere
between a curse and a sigh):
Christmas Daisy!

Sped

Splayed on its back on the footpath: a grey squirrel,
as if dropped, just now, from the scraggy overhanging trees;
mouth fallen agape, yellow cartoon incisors,
the top ones darker, tinged with a raspberry stain.

No sign of damage, creamy fur of the belly
shading to a milky brown tuft — it's a he — one dark eye
almost grazing the concrete, forepaws curled,
their little grappling hooks

hooked to the air, the ghost of a last branch:
the flipside, what it deposits at our feet like a gift,
his luxuriant streamer — so soft you'd want to stroke it —
stirring a little in the backwash from passing cars.

Funny Peculiar

that I, the class dunce,
got bored enough in maths to actually attempt
the sum which Múinteoir Máire had warned us
was difficult, and found to my amazement
the formula began to work, a knot
magically unpicking itself —

that, five years later, dropped out, dandering with a friend
along the edge of a little wood, a place
we often came to, we heard
then saw them: two men striding towards us
like farmers across a field, jackets and ties
in the long-grassed evening, carrying (here I might have blinked)
what appeared to be guns,
a machinegun cradled by the older, limping one
while the other, steadier, held what looked like a handgun —

that when she asked for the answer and no one
possessed it, and I half-raised
a tentative hand and gave it, she demanded coldly:
'Who did you copy that from?' —

that when we heard the man with the machinegun
growl 'I'll fucking kill you'
it moved us to make for the trees but not too fast
since evening, still breathing evenly,
might be persuaded to hold its peace, its pace —

that neither I nor anyone else challenged Múinteoir Máire
(though I dreamed of seeking her out, loading
and aiming that point-blank memory between her eyes)
so I went back to being
what I probably would have been anyway
for the rest of my schooldays and some time beyond
and now she is safely dead
and now she is safely dead —

that before they told us they were Special Branch
(security for the British Embassy Residence whose patch
we'd been trespassing on),
when the calmer man shoved my head hard against a tree,
twisting long hair, pressing into my temple
the steel nub, while he frisked (showed how it felt
to be felt up by death),
                              it put me
into a skin, a voice that could ask coldly:

'What are you going to do with us?'

Lillian's Dream

Alone in the kitchen, she heard, from the living room,
the sound of nobody putting a record on,
followed by the knock on the door
she knew she shouldn't open but had to

on her friend whose mouth opened
to scream and scream

as Lillian felt herself gently pulled back, worked
by the dream-puppetry, into
a far corner to see

what her friend was screaming at: Lillian
hanged dangling from the light-cord,
eyes shut, broken-record-voice the voice
of all our troubled sleeps:

are my eyes open / are my eyes open / are my eyes

Neary's

Half a lifetime since we met for the first
and last time in a crowded pub, our talk,
like the cigarette smoke, layered and dispersed;

like ourselves, lifted on a draft
of faint perfume and pheromones,
into the alley. She mentioned a flight (a path

uncrossed: off my map, east or west or south).
And her number? And if? And when? She sealed
such questions with her silencing mouth.

Nope, I Haven't Yet Figured Out What Beauty Is For
— a response to Mary Oliver

Sure, your wild geese can drag me willy-nilly
with a choked sob into their sky

and I agree that dogs, swans, mockingbirds and doe-eyed stones
deserve to have souls,

but sometimes I want to shout (since a stone can not)
that these have as much need of souls

as the butterfly has of a pin, the biologist's mouse
of the human ear cloned on its back;

that to pile onto furry things spiritual quilts patched
out of wounded rapture

can chill rather than warm, make a soul's teeth chatter
for those others with hardly a stitch:

sea cucumbers, viruses, space junk — the rice grain that fell
from a bird's skull-socket, curled

and writhed in my palm as if butting the swell
of this too-living wall.

Unanswers

Looking for god is like asking directions for the edge of the earth.
— STEPHEN HAWKING

In the beginning there was nothing, which exploded.
— TERRY PRATCHETT

Before the Big Bang, no time, so no room for god
crushed against solid Nothing. We should
be 'pretty pleased'. No need to fear god now
(though what scares most of us, surely, is that paler shadow

at the back of our group photo of devils and gods).

*

At the quantum level we've seen a photon pop
into existence from nothing — why not
'the ultimate free lunch'? So something has come
of nothing: my appetite's gone. Bear with me

Flying Spaghetti Monster made of string theory.

*

The unnameable was always a human name
even as it shrank from having a finger put on it —
sunbeam touching the nerve in a passage tomb,
god of the minded gap, the sucked thumb,

cloud of unknowing breathed on a window pane.

*

What if god comes with the bubble-wrap, fold
between universes, blacker than black rose
bundled into the mother of all black holes?

What if time is a sliced pan, each moment
self-preserved, fresh as the day it was born?

Moseying along that path at the edge of the cliff —
agnostic heartbeat: *what if, what if, what if*

Stopping For The Twelve Apostles
— *On The Great Ocean Road, Australia*

So this is where the land goes
south: pink crumbling stacks,
geology on speed, earth-clouds.

So fast when one of them dropped
its brittle link with the mainland —
'London Bridge' fallen to

'London Arch' — the abrupt island
supported a population: two
startled tourists on hold

for a helicopter. Pointing cameras
into the wind's wall, we snap
oblongs of grandeur

(bite-sized, as befits
this misnomer: the twelve
eroded to eight). As if

such balconies need a wardrobe
of pantomime robes and fake beards
while the older names are still

nodding at us — The Sow
and Piglets, Place Of Many Heads —
up close and at bay

as the many-headed file
that shuffles past, clicks, turns
like a turnstile, except for

this couple in hoodies (hers
a kind of hooded coat
more like a blanket)

huddled together on the rim
of the flashes and grins,
wind-buffeted, slightly desperate

to pocket each other, backed
into the guardrail — as south
as you can get, having unpacked

that portable bedroom wall,
all
the landscape that matters.

High Rise Squat, 1989

A crowbar, that was the thing,
as if I was prising the lid
off a crate, rather than climbing
into a crow's nest for a stowaway.

Across the Channel — the street party
to end all parties — Berlin
was tearing itself together: *Go over and see.*
I kept my head down, stayed in,

fixed a great plastic sheet
in the smashed window: days
that sagged, at peace, or wind, rain, sleet
snapped and rattled my sail.

Found a girlfriend instead of my feet
(so no need to pull up my socks).
Six months, a blink, an age:
skies packing and unpacking while the blocks

stood around us like luggage.

The Tents

A little word, as practical as why,
unpacked itself and came to occupy

a sentence. It began to take up space
and found itself a nylon carapace —

a growing cluster, bright and cellular,
as if directed by a branch of air.

Speeches and rain: the weather has been busy.
Between the streetlights and CCTV

intelligence is gathering. Something waits
that doesn't need to rattle at the gates.

A single torch-beam rolls its eye. All's quiet.
The tents are temporary but not quite.

Stolpersteine

Someone is at work, prising out paving stones.
The work looks proper, official, though he is wearing
a cement-dusted leather cowboy hat.

Someone has made space for something, a little block capped
with brass, a square palm-print outside one
of the houses of the nameless.

Someone has done his homework: HIER WOHNTE _____
a name, date, whatever's available and
can be packed.

Someone has hammered in, punched each letter and number,
each dent in the silence of the clean sheet,
each word ringing with blows.

Someone has laid it in your tracks, something to stumble on:
a street testing its voice, ghost of a shine,
blind spot flickering off.

---

* *Stolpersteine*: 'Stumbling Blocks': German artist Gunter Demnig's ongoing project: memorialising those murdered in the Holocaust by setting plaques outside the houses they originally lived in. His website is www.stolpersteine.com

The Rice Lady

While The Rice Lady can write
your name on a grain of rice
every bullet
has Everyone's name on it.

New York Stopover, 1966

At 93, she recalls what I don't: steam
blooming from pavements —

(loud crack in the afternoon and immediately
the steep up-and-down wail
of American sirens, faces half-borrowed from movies:
the lean dark-haired man in the rumpled shirt
muscled out in handcuffs — cursing?
someone has put him on mute — the older, inert
jewellery-shopkeeper on a stretcher,
passers by passing, sirens again, the incident
gathering itself and rolling off
to curve round a different bend on the same circuit)

— the same steam
                     I woke to a decade later immersed
in *Taxi Driver*'s neon-and-brimstone.

The Crawling Hand

Was a trailer for a B movie
we never saw — one of The Carlton's
coming attractions, after which we sat through

whatever we'd been taken to —
*It's A Mad, Mad, Mad, Mad World,
The Longest Day, Dr No* —

But it was the hand took hold.
Long after O'Connell Street trailered off
with its diesel and daylight, touch

of those tingly words brought a rush
of whispers. Lights out. If we needed a prop
we might take a torch or candle

and float a palm slowly down, till
its claw-fingered shadow caged the whole room.
So we summoned the cast

of monochrome faces aghast
at something approaching, a palpable edge to our lives:
closer, closer, close

as that pocket of dim blue smoke,
popcorn, ice cream, a melting Star Crush,
eyes hatched between sticky fingers — inside

and over our heads the plush dark filming us.

Time Piece

Nothing on the windowsill in her bedroom
but this faceless mantel clock: a boxed porthole
looking straight through itself to capture a round

of net-curtained window. Where did I see it last —
on the upright piano? Why did she move it here?
And where did its face go? No need to ask

the time being perfectly kept.

Present Continuous

Going on two months after you're dead
and I am still saying 'good morning mum'
and before closing the door on what was your room
(dark at first and now full of the lingering

spring evenings) 'good night'.
Presumably death is where time stops
so an afterlife might see past and present locked
in the same room. I ache to see you again

but what will we do with our selves
and the rest of our loved ones floating in the ether?
Beam eternal love at each other
while the cosmos falls apart and flickers out?

From here, it seems rather more likely that what-
ever-we-wish-to-call-it
will spare us all that. No matter. Drop
the odd hint if you can — a song, a smile

in a passing dream — and when I begin to die
fool me, be there waving furiously
door-framed inside that light-flooded
telescopic tunnel at the end

of the last fizzling neuron. See you then.

Primaries

Blue

is what we ascend to

as the seatbelt light pings off and the drinks trolley
squeaks down the aisle: wavelengths scattered like snow
over the napped levels outside / inside
the sun's romper room —

the white ink well's darkly perfect O,
tension of feint-ruled lines, wires
waiting for the scratch of a nib, a slippery Biro —

held breath of warm summer dusk that carries
a mood: smoky laughter, near / distant
as a field holler, a low
lengthening note

that finds you.

Red

is our risen and sunk star, its rumpled bed spread
to extinction —

red-shifted starlight, a lipsticked *GET LOST*
across your face in the mirror —

DEFCON 1, blood in the washbasin —
those things we do not

dwell on, and those we do, a fresh-plucked
tomato, earthily sweet —

deckchair siestas, pulp of a midsummer pressed
on your closed eyelids —

the flowering parts of us, nipped opening bud

of the unsaid.

Yellow

is what the gorse, in spring, bellows —

Joseph Mallord William Turner's breakfasts
on canvas, his *Sunrise With Sea Monsters* ———

a lemon for invisible ink or a measure of the old
heat, spiked with cloves —

broad Gothic shafts flooding a darkened lounge-bar
dazzling the flat-screened soccer
to a dull roar —

what gives to the city's shut face
gratis, these armfuls of ore

and invites it to stretch, wallow.

White

is at the base of life's
wateriness, its never-quite
filled-in page, what resonates

between a and y — vapour trail

of hopes and prayers high
as cumuli — thinned to a
singular line, a sprite.

Black

— *Ivory black, Mars black, Lamp black* —

is, as any painter knows,
never only or merely black

any more than the blackbird still sprinkling its song
over Belfast Lough —

blackboards where a chalky duster has swept
impatient inroads —

zero blackness of space that is nothing
without the stars' itch —

self-dissolve of print, of words' gritty
transparency —

reflective widening pools at the centre
of her eyes as she takes you — or

leaves you — Ivory black, Mars black, Lamp black

The Reverse
— *Cornelius Gijsbrechts, 1670*

Although his trompe l'oeil, 'The Reverse
of a Painting', is intended to deceive,
one double-take is all it takes to leave
the expected for the micro-universe:

nested rectangles, the frame's pale grain, the buff
canvas stretched and pinned with tiny tacks,
the price on a ticket fixed with sealing wax —
range-findings, star-charts, more than enough.

Beyond a trick then, his scrupulous look
at what is overlooked — details that wait
behind what hangs in MoMA or The Tate —
lifted the world of appearance off its hook,

turned it to the wall and then applied
equal pressure to the other side.

Tweet

ever clever
in all weathers
Paul Klee's Twittering
Machine's perched
on a hurdy-gurdy
tickling tree
in the forest
of feathers

Paintings In A Room

should hang true
as mirrors or windows

to be turned to

between the reversed shadows
the stuff seen through.

For Goya's Dog

What parapet, brackish swell, beach, firmament, ark
are you poking your head above?

What are you staring at? Some missing part
of the mural, a bat or dove

in a high corner of Heaven that fell off
when they moved it?

Or is this scoured, vapourish emptiness all
he intended: pit

of despair spreading like damp, a Turneresque stain
framed on the upper floor

of the Quinta Del Sordo — though some say it is not certain
there *was* an upper floor

when your master lived there —

Lost Lens

i.m. Anthony Glavin

A new telephoto, somewhere in the gorse hills
above The Silver Tassie lounge-bar
and that bridge — beautiful

high, arched stonework (bullet-holed
from one of our wars). Clouds
blued into nightfall, rolled

over our desultory poking. Later, I told
my old friend (gone now
nine years) and I can still

see him, smiling, droll:
'Imagine, in a thousand years, someone
will find it and be able to infer

a whole culture.'

Evening Sun, Bullock Harbour

I could watch it for hours, this slight but definite

unstillness. Below the four by fours parked
amidst upturned rowboats where a grey cat prowls,
the tyre-draped wall's honey-coloured blocks

are aquiver with the reflected sea's
gently shifting transparencies, gauzy curtains
in a breeze-ruffled bathroom window,

a dressing and undressing of light.

Tat

— ever been tempted to make
like a scroll, unroll
an intimate exhibition for anyone's eyes —

take time out for
the needle in a strange hand
harrowing your one stretch

of human skin, uncured — be pretty
as a Pict — a name writ
on a passing page that already

amounts to water —

Some Like It

grappling fast and tight
so something desperate as a fire escape
breaks
into each grimace
and coat-hangers and kitchen surfaces
put up a fight

while I don't mind how fast we go
so long as it is slow
enough to feel what sly
gradual surfaces — how the body
holding sway
smiles.

Thigh Gap

Marked by the keen-eyed
who cull the tribe

of what is less
than desirable (presently, flesh),

you ache
for an absence, diamond-shaped

between your legs, hell
of Nothingness in a nutshell.

Nah, take a selfie
of your fuck-off grin, that selkie

you can never quite shed,
who'll tell you when you're being bled

of what you know — the truth:
Beauty is a brute.

Holdall

for Sam

Storm-lashed, safe in a friend's house
deep in a bog above Spiddal,
we weather flaps of sheet lightning,
ripples of muscular dark, spittle
hissing on windows, slates — night arched
so beside and full of itself
it outfleshes the wildest word-cries,
precipitates our sound sleep,

wriggles its way into the creased
morning, post-coffee, as we pack,
bundle clothes, paperbacks, sleepingbags
sweetened with sweat — tomorrow's
holding-together-map stashed
and slung in the boot.

Navels

A good thing to gaze at, your lover's
thimble of dark

•

See you at two, at the deep-shallow pool

•

Vestibule
for nothing more than the tip
of a finger or tongue, graze
of a stranger's guiltless eye

•

A mystery, the way yours is a magnet for fluff

•

Everyone to their own
free-floating punctuation

•

In the window of the tattoo parlour, a photo
of a sailor's encircled by boot-prints
and the words Navel Patrol

•

Forget the skewered eyebrow or chin,
the silver stitch in the lip,
the harpooned tongue —

here's the best place for sinking
that re-engagement ring

•

Stop looking at me there —
it tickles

•

Maybe to say: I exist —
like that bullseye
at the heart of the galaxy —
birth-story with a twist

•

Naba, nabel, navik,
pupak, pupek, pusat, puseg, pusod,

pito, piko, vico, ombelico, ombligo,
umbigo, umbilicus,

innie, outie — this
mammal-mark, shared scar

remembers

•

Vulture Bone Flute
— *38,000 BC*

Fitting to see the oldest airs
salvaged from a raptor — the air
of its wing — and there is music

in our bodies, drums and strings,
wind instruments fulfilling themselves
so blood and sweat sings

to surfaces, half-blinding those eyes
lost in the swing of a scythe,
a notched sword, the haulage

of hominid arms through foliage —
music that runs like sap
back to the root

of our species jogging on the spot
wired to an iPhone — chants, field hollers,
deafening wars, silences — the body

bearing the mind away
with riffs, keys, tones, variations
on what's in us and what will come

to blow through our bones.

Hairpin

Afterwards, I kept finding them
lining the corners of cleared-out drawers.

I picked one up. It was blacker and glossier
than I remember.

Filings, a storm of magnetised particles,
unmagnetised, drift off like leaves.

Total eclipse: you can see the corona's
wild, ungovernable curls.

Cochlear Implant

'I could actually *hear* the skin
separating. I'd peel a hundred satsumas
just to hear that.' And immediately
I wanted to reach for one, dig my thumbs in
for the zesty, whispery rip —

as the inner ear uncoils its stethoscope
for the endangered ghost of a foghorn, tyres
on a wet road's unpeeling tape, the little whinny
a dog sometimes makes in its sleep:

shoes creaking into the fresh snow's crust
in the library of small sounds where satsumas
get peeled very slowly and Basho's frog goes *plop!*
cupped in that haiku, along with its pond
and summer's trembling meniscus.

Boy On A Trampoline

Cocooned by the high
safety fence (a room
for the round air), he space-hops
circling the great hub

of himself — just a step up
from his everyday bounce, moment
by moment laying bare
bed-springs in every floor,

still testing the earth's
suspension, its give — what
grown-ups grow to forget —
gently trampolining even

our heaviest steps.

Notes

ACADEMIC: *page* 17
'The penis is then placed in the vagina' is a line (*the* line) from our school biology book.

ACADEMIC: *page* 18
Translation:
— Did you say anything about *shite*?
— I didn't.
—You did.
— I didn't.
—You did.
— I didn't.

—You did!

—Write it out!

TWO QUESTIONS: *page* 28
'Water bears', or tardigrades or moss piglets, are eight-legged micro-animals that can live in extreme conditions, the first life-forms known to survive (for a little while) in the vacuum of outer space.

A LATE ADDITION TO THE LAMENT: *page* 45
That is, William Dunbar's 16th Century 'Lament For The Makers'. The third line alludes to 'Zen Calvinist' Norman MacCaig's succinct description of his own work as 'either a one or a two cigarette poem.'

UNANSWERS: *page* 60
The Flying Spaghetti Monster is a term that was coined in 2005 to highlight the absurdity of creationist beliefs (i.e. worshipping a creator makes as much sense as believing in a Flying Spaghetti Monster). There is now a Church Of The Flying Spaghetti Monster, and a religion: Pastafarianism.

Mark Granier has published three collections of poetry, *Airborne* (Salmon, 2001), *The Sky Road* (Salmon, 2007) and *Fade Street* (Salt, 2010). His awards include the New Writer Poetry Prize, the Vincent Buckley Poetry Prize and a Patrick and Katherine Kavanagh Fellowship.